grief is a thin place

Lucy Marie

BookLeaf Publishing

India | USA | UK

grief is a thin place © 2023 Lucy Marie

All rights reserved.

No part of this publication may be reproduced, stored in a retrieval system, or transmitted, in any form or by any means, electronic, mechanical, photocopying, recording or otherwise, without the prior written permission of the presenters.

Lucy Marie asserts the moral right to be identified as author of this work.

Presentation by *BookLeaf Publishing*

Web: www.bookleafpub.com

E-mail: info@bookleafpub.com

ISBN: 9789358319323

First edition 2023

For Jack x

ACKNOWLEDGEMENT

To Amy, Emily, Lana, Sasha, Sophie, Yasmin; thank you for surrounding me with wisdom, love, compassion, patience, laughter, strength, and great tits. You are the kind of women who make this world a better place, and I am inspired by you all.

To Jakob, for showing me the kind of love I didn't know I needed and choosing to build this life with me. I love you the same.

For my family, who went to the depths and found their way back up. Thank you for staying the course, for grounding me in love and resilience and music. Thank you for it all.

PREFACE

Maybe I'm ready. Maybe I've finally found the gap where I think I might offer something. Maybe I didn't have time to honour it. Maybe last time I was trying too hard to put it all on paper before I felt it in my bones. Maybe it still hurts too much to let in how much this place means, how much I find him here, in words, and everything beautiful; in people trying, bare-ing their souls; bearing, in the small, prosaic, daily practices. In the music and the train rides. In the streets that somehow stretch all the way back to a time before he died.

And now, I'm required to uphold my end of this relationship, in the only ways I can. Figuring out how to do this without him is, unsurprisingly, harder than, say, phoning a friend. But I choose this hard thing because I feel him upholding it too. Death parts but does not end.

I am grateful to so many speakers on this subject for their honesty and words of understanding – the validation that what I believe is not even original is immeasurably comforting.
Early on I wrote, rather glibly, that grief is like a mortgage I'm still paying off. Now I actually

have a mortgage, I'm not sure the metaphor stands. I won't ever own my grief outright, nor will I be able to trade it in for a four-bed house with a conservatory, nor will I be rewarded with a comfortable retirement for paying it off. It is not separate from me, but rather grows as I do. It ages with me; requiring my care and attention. I am responsible for it and exhausted by it and attached to it in ways I cannot fully fathom nor explain.

There are many things I cannot explain.

For example:

Sometimes you do not long to be comforted.

The following words are there to give you room to feel something else.

syllables

Immaculate pain.
The once raging light; silenced.
Grief has too many

Before it settles

It shook through us like an atom bomb, and we sat there, dust. Let me crack open this skull of mine and let you peer through into the abyss. Drives its nail right into the bone. The screams have never needed translating. And aren't we all stumbling, tumbling, desperate and aflame with need. The sound of a piano. Until all you had were regurgitations. The sound of a piano somewhere. A windowless room still felt too much like letting something in. We weren't ready yet. Snow falls so slowly, so slowly, even in a blizzard - it is only the wind that blows. Did you ever think about that? Did you ever think? We would barter with the devil to get it back. Our crest would have been the stars and the sea, constant and ever changing. A nod to the fire and the baptism that took place when you let it sink in. She would have crucified them all if she'd had the power in her hands. I would have killed them with my bare teeth. And what do I do with my face now? He wouldn't. He did something stupid. Thank you for the lasagne. I hate it. He's gone. I'm swallowing yoghurt. The snow.
So, would you like a cup of tea?

Are we in bloom?

You said
some things shatter, some things bloom.
You forgot the part where the things that shatter
are often the things that bloom best.
All their radiant edges
flowers filling the gaps.

Found

I, young and vulnerable:
my father gave me some advice.
"Remember this world you've had."
He didn't say any more, but I understood.

The mind is secret,
wild,
unknown,
most unmistakable for its intimate revelations
or at least,
the marred judgements of infinite hope.

I am still a little afraid of missing something.

My father and I repeat
a fundamental tolerance.
I come to a limit.
I care what it's founded on.

When I came back last autumn, I wanted the
world to be
sort of
forever;
I want no more.

Autumn

I dreamt the things I was afraid of
seemed suddenly no more alarming
than the wintering of things.

The aging bark,
weathered and unfazed –
so, too, I stood –
no more aghast or grieved by what once seemed
amiss
- now seeming nothing,
but the falling of the leaves.

A Thin Place

My whole life has been a game of Operation;
or the game you played in the doctor's office
with the snaking metal wire
- just stay within the lines.

Most days,
my whole being seems to vibrate like that
shaking metal loop.
I'm just trying to pass through.

These days, I've got so good at keeping steady
I forgot what stillness was.

And then you,

you were

exquisite
stillness

except, perhaps

I know you well enough by now to know

that most days

you are exquisitely alive with this constant
humming too.

Yet somehow, the static settles
when I melt into your arms.
Or when I place even one of my palms in the
square of your back;
something that can only be described as a
chemical reaction.

Maybe it is like someone said

for every action there is an equal and opposite
reaction

or

like how sound waves can be dampened by foam
egg boxes

or

how ocean breakers keep the sea inside itself

or

like how destructive interference is when two
sound waves with different frequencies overlap
and the noise level or volume actually decreases.

I've always loved when poetry and science
overlap.

At least I hope this is the way it feels for you.

Two pebbles dropped with perfect precision into
the middle of a lake
cause ripples
that upon finding each other take on the shape of
one another.

When my skin meets your skin, it takes on the
shape of something that can only be described
as

And I am reminded that the edges of this body
that works so hard to keep me inside myself
are temporary.

And your touch is the thin place.

Poor Ophelia

When sorrows come, they come not in single
spies but in battalions,
except she said
battle lions
and we have never laughed so hard.

If only we knew then,
how right she was.

Expand

If you are severed, completely
from yourself,
in a way you never thought possible,
after all the years and work,
If you are salt-sodden, wrecked and restless,
and the sound of time healing
makes you want to claw
and ruin and roar
If it is all you can do
to stand in the naked bathroom light
and sob
and sip water, gingerly
and go back to bed, heavily
If you cannot swallow yoghurt
and chewing aches
and your face is all wrong
If your confidence is gone
because the solid truths you based yourself upon
have disintegrated into dust
and it seems like too much
to trust any of your judgements ever again
If the dust has crept in
and blanketed the carpet
If the carpet has been a good place
to lay awhile

If the thought of next year makes you sick
If the thought of changing the channel makes
you sick
If the thought of that thing you had planned,
the one that was good, and supposed to be good,
makes you sick
If you are shocked at your own hunger
and want to find ways to punish or suppress it
If you have laughed and been overthrown by a
guilt so profound
you might die alongside them
If you don't remember who you have told
or what you have told them
and the nights are unfathomable
and they are calling you brave
and it makes you afraid
and you can't find your words or your breath or
your name.

Look for the place
where the veil is thin
where ten years can pass
in the blink of an eye
and the expanse is enough
to contain all that they were
and all you've become
and let it be rough, awash with your breathtaking
grief
and let it begin.

That Middle Place

The truth, I've found,
is that all of us are challenged to live our lives in
middle,
between what was
and what is, now
and what we ached for it to be.

Departure

How blunt,
our unrequited ache for nescience;
knowing all too well one moment altered you,
and is doing so for eternity;
how cruel, the impalpable thief
who steals you from an innocence you never
knew you loved.

See here:
your chest, hollowed
as if one's heart forgot itself,
and left you with the emptiness a part of you
feared would always come.
See the mind unspool
as it confronts the bittersweet knowing
that we enter alone
and remain so.

Any company that chooses to bless us for this
long and arduous journey home
is a Grace
we do not deserve
and an impossible resource,
without which, all else is lost.

How is this life, no more than a yearning,
which begins with being thrust into the light,
nascent,
and ends with the fall.

What they don't tell you about moving

I am confronted by the unfathomable wholeness
of myself

and the raw fear-soaked truth that
-yes -
this too muchness
that I have always felt, is in fact woven into the
very fabric of the way this living works.

This is all too much to understand.

The entirety of me is incomprehensible to
anyone that hasn't sifted through this minutiae
and understood each letter and touched each gel
pen and felt a thousand memories, and held each
miscellaneous piece of paper and thereby seen
my soul.

I'm not even sure the entirety of me is
comprehensible to me most days.

You could look at a photo. I could show you my
young, plain face and you would remember
something like youth, empathy.

But what about this stone
And this string
And this ribbon

What about these gloves and those hula
necklaces and these keys that might open a flat I
once fought death in.

I am unknowable in all the details

the mountain of my life laid out looks like
electric plugs and buttons and an old camera and
a night light

but it feels like - something I can't even put my
words to.

And it sickens me

because

I could let you read the notebooks and you
would know your own angst, the bad teenage
poetry we all wrote.

But the ticket stubs and the wooden letters of my
name are spilling over with the life and the
breath of me

and

I can see her in a way that no one ever saw me

in a way no one could

but I can't give that to you.

I can't show you the whole picture of myself.
And let you know me that way I think I should
be known.

It is immeasurable.

All the dreaming and the aging

and the fact that I have accidentally documented
it all like I knew I'd need proof of myself one
day.

Like telling you a story was never going to be
enough to make sure you really knew

because I need you to know me
because if you know me and tell me I'm ok

then I'm ok.

Like I knew one day I'd want to put my hands
around the grief I have accumulated and choose
to throw it out
or keep it.

They don't tell you loss is an achievement.

You don't feel it.

But here is an insurmountable box of me.

And I am everything, all at once.

And I am always imagining my mother's hands
going through all of his things and wondering
who he was, and why it is.

And what you might one day have to do with
all this stuff and things of mine.

And it is too much.

Grief has no eyes.

I am just a stomach some days.
Grief sits me down,
the whole vortex,
onto the grass,
and I starve.

I am realising that grief is the one with legs.
An absurdity
that walks shoeless
and sockless and naked -
pasty, hairy calves, thick toenails:
a giant.

No one laughs.

I think it is outrageous,
and vulgar,
except I mustn't.

I am just a head poking out of a cardboard box,
carried by a giant,
below me the void, I think are guts.

Maybe the sides of my mouth are hungry
but chewing takes time and teeth.

And grief doesn't have a tongue
or patience.

So no one laughs.

Once, I began to grow fond,
familiar perhaps.
Indentations appear in its limbs where I rest my
chin.
The scenery around me changes.

This whole thing; absurd,
to get so used to something monstrous...

When it does come
the first laugh is painful.
Grief shrinks.
A little light flickers somewhere.
It is shame and embarrassment.

For the first time, I see grief has no eyes
it has carried me this far; without thanks,

without knowing what I might become.

Rescue

Sometimes the answer
is simply to let people love you.
To receive it
as though it were the only love they had.

So when the rescue doesn't come
or maybe does
your heart is broken soft and open
ready
to translate the all or nothingness
into something else.

Something you can use
and keep
and cherish
transcend
until the act and the intention
meet, part
return
deliver

Enchanted

There is joy and wonder,

and then there is the sullen look of her small
face,
as she crouches behind the statue of Cezanne I
am trying to photograph,
too much in my way to be coincidental,

and the cadence of a street below a window;
the feel of one socked foot against the other.

There is hope that bursts its seams and leaves us
wrecked.
The sweetness of slowly brewed tea and wine
drunk lazily in big gulps.
The evening air, as it cools, and then the delight
of warm, soft things pulled on and over.

There is water, too warm,
and the angle of their shoulders against the sun,
the roots that climb beyond us;

the colour of tomatoes,
the dull disappearance of a headache,
the fervour of hunger, then abated.

There was always joy and wonder,

but I have found myself enchanted,
by this life after death;

Grief has me enchanted.

For now I search – am always searching –
for the essence of him.

Often, it is a quality of light, or sound,
like an artist's impression, or the echo
underneath a bridge by that childhood lake,

some subtle imprint,
on this vast, impossible world he left us with.

Bedtime Poems 24/10/23

For years, my life was a liminal space
a silky river
that connected the Before, to an After
I wasn't certain of
and hadn't quite reached yet.

When I learned to meditate,
I was told to pay attention to the space just
before the exhale.

There, you will find, nothing happens.

It is a granular detail, barely noticeable.
The trick is not to hold or force it either,
the aim is not to reproduce a pattern,
or count,
but observe it in your natural breath.
It can be found at both ends,
in between the exhale and the inhale,
but I started with the top.
The stillness found here
clung like droplets to each other on a glass.

For years, and years,
almost a decade of them,

my life was lived in this space.
Instead of crossing over,
I swam in the inky waters,
back and forth.
Sometimes, so far back, I almost reached the
start.
But the currents pull one way.

Sometimes, I think I have reached the After,

only to crawl up onto this littoral land,
on hands and knees and turn,
toward the light glinting on what I now know
is a lake.

Here, I lie awake,
listening for the soundless air
between the sounds that keep me from the sleep,
I crave
the brush, the hum, the purr and whine, the
rattle, the clamour, the muted stereophonic echo,
the whistling shout, the unruly thud,
and in between:
the sound the moon makes,
the silence,

the velvet, whispered silence.
I was trained for this.

I fill my lungs with the air between the brittle
noise,
fill my whole chest,
fill my belly,
my head,
I inhale, until there is no more breath to take,

then slip, silently,
back into the water.

For you

sleep. bone-weary one
until such stuff as dreams
appear like waking hours
and the heaviness that comes
from the burning of the wick
of your soul to feed the daylight -
releases you
into a thousand sighs
that escape
and take flight -

and take the sweet route home
to yourself
and take time

sleep. until the wax dries
and the insurmountable night
cracks
into a thousand shards of sunlight
that whistle and soar
and beckon
and pierce the canvas of your skin
filling you with whatever firelight
is filled with.
that hazy glow -

of witchcraft.

and rest; until the ash is blown away -
on an exhale that is longer than the last breath -
until you feel the rising
and can't imagine what else you would do
but follow it.

Birthday

Bring me your celebratory ghost,
in a 3am dream
the corners of sheet cake
the passing of light
the longer route home.

Give me the height of that cliff face
gift-wrapped, hand-picked
the depths of your soul.

Bring me balloons
the actual moon
the actual sound of your voice as it was
the colour of wine
the wish that I lost.

Nothing will do.

Send me tomorrow
the snow
long distance calls.

And hand-written love.

Let there be

candlelight and
the hymn with my name.

And I will learn how
to treasure the darkness,
that comes with my breath,
that came with your last.

All over again.

How to live

With joy, they said.
So I picked up a book,
read the manual front to back
picked up a pen,
regurgitated it
wrote reams of joyful words on pages.
Ate fruits and things were green;
I cleaned.

www.ingramcontent.com/pod-product-compliance
Lightning Source LLC
LaVergne TN
LVHW010934200726
843509LV00013B/2221

9 7 8 9 3 5 8 3 1 9 3 2 3